BOOKS BY

REYNOLDS PRICE

PRIVATE
CONTENTMENT

REYNOLDS PRICE

PRIVATE CONTENTMENT

A PLAY

NEW YORK

ATHENEUM

1984

Copyright © 1984 by Reynolds Price
All rights reserved
Published simultaneously in Canada by
McClelland and Stewart Ltd
ISBN 0–689–11455–9
Library of Congress catalog card number 83–45523
Composition by Heritage Printers, Inc.,
Charlotte, North Carolina
Manufactured by Fairfield Graphics,
Fairfield, Pennsylvania
Designed by Harry Ford
First Edition

FOR

JEFFREY ANDERSON

Private Contentment was conceived in response to a commission from WNET-Channel 13, New York. The job was to produce a ninety-minute play for television broadcast in the "American Playhouse" series on PBS. I wrote it in the summer and early fall of 1981. Though it is set in North Carolina, it was filmed on location in South Carolina in February 1982 and was first shown throughout the country on 27 April 1982.

The text printed here is nearly identical with the production script—differing only in the restoration of a few cuts, in a handful of minor matters affected by weather and other exigencies of filming, and in the odd small verbal change.

At its first printed appearance, may I suggest that the play would also lend itself to the stage? With the possible omission of scenes 9 and 14, the insertion of an interval after scene 13, the use of a fluid set, and a strict refusal by all parties to purvey the stereotypes of the stage-South, these characters and their actions would move quite naturally into the theater.

R. P.

CHARACTERS

SGT. DI LUCCA—*a large Italo-American, mid- to late 20s*

LOGAN MELTON—*age 20, sensibly built but vulnerable*

THE CHAPLAIN—*mature with the businessman-air of Protestant clerics*

TEE—*black, late 30s, a harder edge than the traditional maid*

PAUL MELTON—*age 45, clearly once-handsome with strong remnants of his young magnetism. A decent man in possession of numerous sealed and dangerous compartments*

MR. APPLEGATE—*mid-50s, a furniture dealer*

LENA BROCK—*age 38, self-possessed but capable of surprise*

DAYTON
ADELE } *sixth-grade pupils, age 12*
TALLER BOY

GAIL BROCK—*age 14, lovely with the trace of a resemblance to* LOGAN

EXTRA—*two men on street (one black), schoolchildren, the driver of a car*

PLACES

A military base in Idaho and eastern North Carolina

TIME

March 1945

PRIVATE CONTENTMENT *was first presented by "American Playhouse" on PBS, 27 April 1982, with the following cast:*

(IN ORDER OF APPEARANCE)

LOGAN MELTON	*Peter Gallagher*
SGT. DI LUCCA	*Mark Zimmerman*
THE CHAPLAIN	*Dan Nelson*
TEE	*Beatrice Winde*
PAUL MELTON	*John McMartin*
MR. APPLEGATE (MR. JEFFCOAT in the first production)	*Laurens Moore*
LENA BROCK	*Kathryn Walker*
GAIL BROCK	*Trini Alvarado*

Directed by VIVIAN MATALON
Produced by SAM PAUL *and* LINDSAY LAW
Associate Producer SUSIE SIMONS
Director of Photography PETER STEIN
Art Director HOWARD CUMMINGS
Costume Designer EDI GIGUERE
Film Editor DOUG CHEEK
Music composed by JAMES TAYLOR

PRIVATE
CONTENTMENT

1

A barn of a recreation room in Officers' Quarters, U.S. Army. Idaho; late afternoon.

The hand of a young man suspends above a keyboard— old piano ivory. The fingers are slowly rehearsing in the air.

Then an unseen voice from some yards behind—

SGT. DI LUCCA
Make it sweet, Lieutenant.

The hand descends and begins to play the simplest great music, Bach's Prelude in C.

After three measures we see the whole man, earnestly recalling the piece. He is twenty, with spacious calm features and distinction in his eyes.

The heavy-set sergeant approaches through the room, then stops to listen.

4

After ten measures the right hand misstrikes a note and stops. The lieutenant turns to face DI LUCCA, *smiling.*

LOGAN

Maybe I'll do better under Nipponese fire.

DI LUCCA

I hope you get the chance, sir.

LOGAN

(*Thinks a moment, stands*) Have I overlooked a duty?

DI LUCCA

You're wanted by the chaplain, sir.

LOGAN

Hell, he wants us *all*.

DI LUCCA

Not me, sir. He's terrified of Catholics. (*Grins*) Join us.

LOGAN

Where do I sign?

DI LUCCA *extends a hand and* LOGAN *mock-signs it.* DI LUCCA *studies his palm, then wipes it on his trouser-leg.*

DI LUCCA

You got to see him, sir. On the double, I think.

LOGAN

(*Fans his arms, helpless*) He's the bad-news man.

(*Looks quickly out a sunny window—more soldiers walking*) Well, thanks. Maybe thanks.

LOGAN *trots toward the door. The moment he vanishes—*

DI LUCCA

Maybe you're welcome.

2

Ten minutes later the CHAPLAIN'*s office. The stout bald* CHAPLAIN *sits behind a desk.* LOGAN *sits on his left, telephone in hand. He has talked with his father for several minutes now.*

LOGAN

Did she have any warning? (*We do not hear his father's replies, only* LOGAN'*s spaced questions and final promise*) Was she in much pain? . . . Was anybody with her? . . . I'm glad of that much . . . The chaplain says I can get a week's leave. Now I have to hop a flight. That may take a day or two. . . Are you all right? . . . I'll *be* there, Dad. (*Hangs up slowly and sits back stunned*) This morning she was sitting with the maid in the kitchen and bent to pick up a spoon off the floor. The maid said she got the spoon and clutched it but never sat up. She just kept gently going on down till she'd laid herself out. Then she hit her forehead one time with her fist. (*Repeats her action*)

CHAPLAIN

A stroke. A great blessing.

LOGAN

(*Thinks, then stands*) Sir, it would take more time than I've got to understand that. (*Moves toward the door, then turns*) She was still a young woman.

CHAPLAIN

(*Nods*) You loved her, I'm sure. (*Waits*) Shall we pray?

LOGAN

No sir.

3

LOGAN'S *hometown in North Carolina, two evenings later, falling late-winter light.* LOGAN *has driven* TEE, *the family cook, home at the end of the funeral day.*

Though TEE *is only forty, straight and strong,* LOGAN *helps her from the car and walks beside her uphill toward the house.*

When they reach the steps, TEE *stops and faces him. She still wears her mourning dress and hat.*

                    TEE
You all right, aren't you?

                    LOGAN
(*Nods*) Tired.

                    TEE
How many days you got to rest?

                    LOGAN
Five, maybe four. (*Smiles*) Then I might invade Japan.

TEE

Don't scare people, Logan. It's been a bad week.

LOGAN

(*Nods*) I'll be shipped out any day. You may have another funeral to cook.

TEE

(*Firmly lays her palm on his lips*) Don't say that anywhere your daddy can hear.

LOGAN

He never needed me.

TEE

You're what he's *got* now.

LOGAN

(*Smiles*) Uncle Sam's got me. Don't lean on me.

TEE *reaches to stop his mouth again, but* LOGAN *takes a step back in gathering darkness.*

4

Ten minutes later, the cemetery. LOGAN *steps from the car and walks toward his mother's grave. The funeral wreaths, left hours ago, are startlingly fresh.* LOGAN *stands a long moment, looking down. He bends, takes one red rose and smells it, then speaks to his mother.*

LOGAN
I can honestly say I'm sorry you're gone. But please—I don't want to join you, not yet. Help me through what's coming. I want a whole life. (*Puts the rose to his mouth, then throws it gently to the grave*) I'm sorry you didn't but I already said that.

He turns toward the car.

5

A quarter-hour later, the kitchen of LOGAN's *family home. His father,* PAUL MELTON, *is seated at a clean table, a glass of bourbon before him. He is forty-five, a little fatigued but still firm and focused in body and eyes. At the sight of* LOGAN, PAUL *points to a cupboard.*

PAUL

You want to pour it?

LOGAN

(*Moving to the cupboard*) Thank you, I can.

Through the start of their talk, LOGAN *finds ice cubes and pours a stiff glass of unwatered bourbon. He leans on a counter, facing his father but some yards distant.*

PAUL

You stop by Marian's?

LOGAN

No sir, I spoke to her outside the church.

PAUL

I hoped you might have more to say to her.

LOGAN

(*Smiling but earnest*) Dad, I'm in the midst of a little task called World War II. If I concentrate, I may outlast it with all my parts. Then I'll start back listening to anybody offering plans for my life.

PAUL

You'll be all right.

LOGAN

You write to Hirohito? He promise to spare me?

PAUL

(*Smiles*) They don't, as a rule, wipe a whole family out. They wouldn't take you right after your mother.

LOGAN

"They" are running this baby a whole new way.

PAUL

(*Points to a chair at the table beside him, but* LOGAN *stays in place*) You're saying you're scared?

LOGAN

(*Nods*) You ashamed?

PAUL

(*Thinks, takes a long swallow from his glass*) I guess shame has got very little work from me. (*Faces* LOGAN)

No, I just don't want you boarding a troopship with anything less than a full deck of cards. (*Smiles*) You may need your aces.

LOGAN

That's what *I'm* saying, Dad.

PAUL

Stop wanting them then.

LOGAN

Sir?

PAUL

Stop giving a damn.

LOGAN

I'd be dead on the beach.

PAUL

You'd be happy though.

LOGAN

Great Jesus, Dad!

PAUL

(*Grips his glass and stares at the half-inch of bourbon*) Have I had too much? I still can't believe you aren't just off on a Boy-Scout trip.

LOGAN

(*Nods*) It changes now.

PAUL

A lot does, I guess. (*Looks slowly round the room*)

LOGAN

You won't move, will you?

PAUL

This is too much house.

LOGAN

Tee can handle it all. She always has. I doubt Mother ever cooked twenty-five meals.

PAUL

(*Grins*) She made really good cheese sandwiches when I first met her—trimmed off the crusts and fried them in butter. Then she found Tee to help her. Tee knew so much more. Will she be here tomorrow?

LOGAN

Every morning you want her, till Judgment Day.

PAUL

I'll rattle at *night*. (*Looks straight at* LOGAN) You won't ever live here again, do you think?

LOGAN

(*Picks up a cloth potholder from the counter, studies it a moment—his mother's embroidery*) I really can't say.

PAUL

You'll want to finish college—so Christmas and Easter
for two more years, you'd call on me here. Then you'd
be turning out money and babies somewhere up the
line where people want to be. Nobody your age, after
hearing this war, will ever want to live in this much peace
again.

LOGAN

(*Seems to nod, replaces the potholder, takes up his glass,
walks to the table, and sits five feet from his father's
right hand*) Just keep the piano. If I return victorious
from Mount Fujiyama, I may want to sit here and play
for six months.

PAUL

(*Smiles*) I'll keep it tuned and ready.

LOGAN

Then I'll try to be something—a lawyer, I guess.

PAUL

Well, hurry. Your father may need your help.

LOGAN

(*Studies him quickly, decides he's joking*) Hold your
horses another few years. Then I'll give you cut-rates
on a first-class defense.

PAUL *smiles, then stares at his glass in sudden gravity.*

LOGAN

How will you be?

PAUL *seems not to hear.*

LOGAN

Dad, what'll you do?

PAUL *continues staring down but stretches his right hand out toward* LOGAN *and, using his thumb and little finger, walks the hand in quick comic circles; then collapses it, exhausted.*

LOGAN *laughs and leans to pat the hand in mock consolation.*

LOGAN

You entering the postwar Olympics?

PAUL

Just the Great Race of Life—the distance event. Selling pianos and a few church organs through the countryside, deprived as it is. (*Drinks a swallow*) If they still *make* pianos.

LOGAN

Sure they will—

PAUL

They will but will anybody play them again? Won't everybody be out riding like cyclones?

LOGAN

For what?

PAUL

(*Faces* LOGAN, *eyes shining*) Hell, for *joy!* This country's promised *joy.* Now people mean to find it.

LOGAN

Let them. They'll have to stop eventually.

PAUL

—In the ground, when they've burrowed six feet under-
ground.

LOGAN

You've done a lot of riding.

PAUL

Worn myself out.

LOGAN

I always told myself you were happy. When I'd walk in
from a really big day in the fourth damn grade and
Mother and Tee would be sitting right here, both blue
as ink, I'd tell myself "There is one person out there,
happy as me; and he'll be back Friday evening by six."

PAUL

(*Calmer*) What made you think that?

LOGAN

(*Thinks*) The way you'd meet me. You could sell
pianos—or not sell a one—from Monday through Friday on the sizzling roads and still look glad to see a
normal child.

PAUL

That's no big virtue.

LOGAN

Mother asked you once "Who is this tired stranger?"
You said "The truest heart south of Baltimore" and
she said "Welcome!"

PAUL

(*Smiles*) She did what she could. (*Empties his glass
in another long swallow*) You coming with me?

LOGAN

Sir?

PAUL

Tomorrow—I've got to sell *something* this week. Little
two-day trip. You've plumbed Idaho. Now learn the
mysteries of eastern Carolina.

LOGAN

I may not need another mystery this week.

PAUL

(*Thinks, then calmly*) Just people—having daily lives—
nothing too strange.

LOGAN

It's not too soon?

PAUL

For what?

LOGAN

Leaving here, right after a funeral.

PAUL

Let me guarantee this much—we'll miss her all our lives, and what any damned bystander has to say means as much as cold spit.

LOGAN

(*Nods*) What time?

6

The next morning, eight o'clock. LOGAN *opens the front door and steps onto the porch, his shaving kit in hand.*

PAUL *is dimly seen in the hall, speaking to* TEE.

> PAUL
>
> —Tomorrow evening probably, by suppertime. Have something good ready.

> TEE
>
> Have I ever cooked bad?

PAUL *sees the funeral flowers on the door—a spray of white with palmleaf trimmings. He thinks a moment, then sets down his well-used Gladstone bag and carefully lifts the flowers from their nail.*

> PAUL
>
> (*Holding them out*) You want these, Tee?

> TEE
>
> (*Shaking her head*) Bad luck and you know it.

PAUL

(*Smells them slowly, then thrusts them on* TEE) Burn them please. Right now.

7

Three hours later, fifty miles east. A smalltown furniture-store with three pianos against the back wall. PAUL *and* LOGAN *are beside the pianos, talking with the manager—*MR. APPLEGATE.

PAUL
(*Stroking the lid of a dark upright*) We're having a hell of a time with wood—had a whole boatload of mahogany sunk by one torpedo two weeks ago—but I think I can promise you three more uprights and one or two spinets between now and Christmas.

APPLEGATE
Who's going to play them, Paul? There're not enough children round here now to field a team, much less play scales.

PAUL
They'll be back any day. This war's bound to end; and then broad droves of the horniest boys since Greece took Troy will be landing here, pumping out children like rivets and signing them up for piano lessons.

APPLEGATE

I wish I could believe you.

PAUL

(*Looking round for* LOGAN, *who is raising the lid on the sole baby-grand*) There's your proof—my boy there, aching for a chance.

APPLEGATE

(*To* LOGAN, *joking*) I heard they kept you boys supplied with girls, whole tentfuls of ready girls every weekend.

LOGAN

(*Nods, straightfaced*) Yes sir, they do—no extra charge. No music though. It's music we're *craving*.

LOGAN *strikes two chords in heraldry, Da-Dum. Then not sitting down, he starts a slow boogie—elegant and perfect. After ten seconds he breaks off mid-bar, turns, and bows to* APPLEGATE.

LOGAN

(*Mock-serious still*) That's all we boys are fighting for.

APPLEGATE

(*Laughs, claps his hands lightly, then turns to* PAUL) Send me two uprights.

PAUL

And one more spinet?

APPLEGATE

All right.

PAUL *bows toward* LOGAN *and all three laugh.*

8

An hour later, off the main road east. Warm noon sun.
PAUL *and* LOGAN *have stopped by an old bridge across a
small river to eat the lunch* TEE *packed for them. They sit
on the ground on a blanket by the car at the foot of an
oak. They have finished the food and are resting now, on
their backs looking up.*

PAUL
(*Quietly*) It seems like we did this before.

LOGAN
Sir? Did what?

PAUL
Lay back like this—here—years ago. You were out of
school—fourth or fifth grade—and were traveling with
me. We stopped here—trees were green—it was hot—you
were swimming backstroke.

LOGAN
(*Turns to see his father, who does not meet the gaze*)
No sir. Not me. I wish it had been.

PAUL

Your mother was always saying you'd be bored, and I gave in to her.

LOGAN

Maybe she was right but I'm sorry she won—she won a lot, didn't she? Anyhow, I used to stay home and think about you. I didn't exactly have a life myself—just other dumb kids and books to read—so I spent a lot of time making up lives for you.

PAUL

(*Laughs lightly, then turns to look once quickly*) What were they like?

LOGAN

(*Sits up and faces the river*) What you did when you were gone, what you turned into. See, I had to convince myself you didn't just vanish every week when you left me and Mother.

PAUL

Maybe I did.

LOGAN

No, you turned *into* things.

PAUL

(*Smiles, looking up*) Yeah, a hot tired piano salesman, eating pig scraps at crossroad cafés.

LOGAN

A lot more than that.

PAUL

(*Rising on his elbows and searching Logan's face*) Want to tell me what else?

LOGAN

Everything I was scared of—you kidnapped children and were drunk every night; you danced in roadhouses and let women follow you back to cool rooms in dark tourist courts where nobody knew your name.

PAUL

(*Laughs*) How much did that worry you?

LOGAN

Not a bit. It just made me hope for you even harder.

PAUL

(*Lying back again*) When was all this?

LOGAN

Oh, till I was fourteen and had my own secrets.

PAUL

Did you ever tell your mother?

LOGAN

Not a syllable, no. That was my other job—not bothering her.

PAUL

Where did *she* think I was?

LOGAN

(*Studying* PAUL *a moment*) Where you said you'd be, I guess—in country-hotel rooms with one rusty fan and no telephone, reading *True Detective Stories* half the night.

PAUL

Did she have a good time?

LOGAN

When?—thinking of you?

PAUL

In her life—the years you watched her life.

LOGAN

I never much thought so till I hit the army. Not that she seemed like any big tragedy; but blue too much of the time—all the memories she staged on all the anniversaries: her father's stroke, her brother losing half his leg in France on November 10th, 1918. She had a big stock. I'd avoid her those days; but once I hit the army and heard how bad everybody else's mother had been *every day*, then I realized mine had been easy on me.

PAUL

You were good to her.

LOGAN

Everybody else was. She never harmed a soul.

PAUL

Something harmed her though, long before I knew her. Something crushed a part of her that grown people need.

LOGAN

What?

PAUL

(*Thinks*) A hoper, I guess. She lacked normal hopes.
She expected the worst, doubted every good moment.

LOGAN

She was right after all. The worst hit her, broadside.

PAUL

(*Sits up carefully, looks at his shoes, then faces* LOGAN
gravely) That may need explaining.

LOGAN

(*Mildly puzzled*) Dad, she *died*—young as you, four
days ago, neither one of us there. (*By the end he is
visibly moved*)

PAUL

(*Calm*) Tee was with her. Tee held her. Tee said your
mother knew her.

LOGAN

(*Quiet but firm*) That was not good enough.

PAUL

Nothing ever was or will be.

LOGAN *is increasingly moved and angered. He stands
and takes two steps toward the river. When he's calmed
a little, he speaks toward the water.*

LOGAN

Is that the absolute best you've got to raise the spirits
of a poor soldier-boy bound to liberate Asia?

PAUL *thinks, then stands, removes his jacket, and rolls
his sleeves to the elbows neatly.*

LOGAN *turns in the silence and watches, baffled.*

PAUL *smiles to* LOGAN *but walks forward past him, squats,
and carefully washes his hands in the river shallows. His
hands still submerged,* PAUL *looks up to* LOGAN.

PAUL

You ready?

LOGAN

For what?

PAUL

You asked for raised spirits.

LOGAN *does not understand but removes his jacket,
squats by* PAUL *and sinks his own hands in water sur-
prisingly warm for March.*

LOGAN

What warmed it so early?

PAUL

My smoldering heart— (*Smiles to* LOGAN)

LOGAN *faces him gravely.*

PAUL *stirs his right hand, then accurately scoops a full palm of water onto* LOGAN'S *face.*

LOGAN *rises, laughing and brushing himself.*

9

Two hours later, three o'clock, they have pushed on east into flat farmland and tall pinewoods. Their car (LOGAN driving now) threads the main street of a village—six or seven store-buildings, a filling station. The street is empty till they reach the end of buildings.

There two older men are standing at the edge of pavement, talking (one white, one black). They watch as the car nears; and when they see PAUL, the black man raises a hand in silent greeting.

PAUL turns and smiles in response.

                         LOGAN

He own a piano?

                          PAUL

He's the bootlegger, no.

                         LOGAN

Should we patronize him?

PAUL

(*Points forward*) I think I can cover our needs. If not, I know his house.

LOGAN

(*Looks round, incredulous*) We staying *here* tonight?

PAUL

(*Points left for a turn*) We may, we may.

They are now at the absolute end of the town—a few houses to their left, fields to their right.

LOGAN

We sleeping in the fields?

PAUL

(*Smiles*) Hold your horses. (*Points another turn left*)

A two-story schoolhouse, a dirt parking-lot with three or four cars. LOGAN *turns in.*

PAUL

Now stop. (*As they park he studies* LOGAN's *profile*) We made it.

LOGAN

To where?

10

Five minutes later in the big dim hallway of the school,
PAUL *stops at a shut door.* LOGAN *is behind him. The
voices of children singing leak through—the Czarist National Hymn of Russia.* LOGAN *is about to ask a puzzled
question.* PAUL *silences him with a finger held to his own
mouth, then opens the door enough to see a woman lead-
ing the chorus toward a close.*

The CHILDREN—*eleven and twelve years old (all white)—
see* PAUL *first but sing on.*

*Then the woman—*LENA BROCK—*senses a presence and
looks over quickly. She smiles slightly, goes on con-
ducting with her left hand, and comes to the door to
usher* PAUL *in. She is thirty-eight, still winsome with an
undemonstrative force.*

LOGAN *follows, unexpected.*

LENA *smiles but barely conceals her surprise at* LOGAN'S
entry.

PAUL *goes to a side wall and stands as if accustomed to being there.*

LOGAN *follows uneasily.*

LENA *moves toward a small piano at the front of the room (one of* PAUL'S *spinets) and stands there, waving the hymn to its ending.*

LENA

Beautiful, children—the National Hymn of Russia, our strongest ally. And you sang it with no piano at all. What is that called, Dayton?

DAYTON

(*A boy toward the back of the room*) Hard, I guess.

General laughter, a scattered show of hands.

LENA

Adele?

ADELE

A *cappella*, you said.

LENA

And I told you the truth! (*Laughs*)

The end-of-day bell rings loudly in the hall. A few boys rise.

LENA

Don't forget what I said—listen to the news tonight and copy down any big Russian victories. Then we'll learn the *Polish* anthem. Go quietly now.

The CHILDREN *leave in their best semblance of order, a suppressed melee.*

As the last two boys approach LOGAN *at the wall, the* TALLER BOY *seizes* DAYTON *by the hair and pulls his head back.* DAYTON *howls but slips free and stops before* LOGAN.

DAYTON

(*Points to* LOGAN's *insignia*) Can I have your badge?

LENA

Dayton, that's enough—

LOGAN

They'd arrest me without it.

DAYTON

My brother gave me his. *He's* still running loose.

LOGAN *laughs, unfastens a small enameled shield, and hands it to* DAYTON.

DAYTON *studies it a moment, then runs to the door where the* TALLER BOY *waits.*

LENA

Dayton, you forgot.

TALLER BOY

(*Pokes* DAYTON *on the shoulder*) Tell him "Thank you,"
Little Dummy.

DAYTON

I'll make my sister pray for you.

The two boys leave.

LOGAN

(*To their backs*) Tell her "Quick and don't stop."
(*Manages a smile*)

LENA

You should meet his sister. She can half-raise the dead!

*A silent moment while the meaning of that settles round
the three faces.*

PAUL

This is my son, Mrs. Brock.

LENA

—Logan. (*Stays in place behind the piano, not stern
but not smiling*)

LOGAN

Yes ma'm. I liked the song.

LENA

Joe Stalin wouldn't. It's the old Czar's anthem. Our music books are ancient, but I haven't told the children.

PAUL

Don't confuse them.

LENA

(*Still to* LOGAN) I want them to learn all the allied anthems.

LOGAN

You just teach music?

LENA

Oh no, everything but auto repair. What you need to learn?

LOGAN

(*Embarrassed*) It'd take all day.

LENA

School's out. I'm free. (*But looks to* PAUL)

PAUL

How's the new piano?

LENA

(*Patting the lid*) Too good for *me*. (*Steps round, plays a few chords*) One or two bass notes have slipped a little maybe. (*Strikes the notes, slightly sour*) But the children never need them.

PAUL

Those boys' voices will be deepening any day. I'll tune it tomorrow morning early.

LENA *nods, then looks a little shyly toward* LOGAN.

LENA

I know *you* play.

LOGAN

(*Mildly puzzled at her knowledge*) I'm rusty now.

PAUL

Let her hear you.

LOGAN

(*Firmly to* PAUL) Not now.

For a moment they face each other, debating the need for a wrangle.

LENA *rises from the bench.*

PAUL *relents and turns to her.*

PAUL

We'll take you home.

LENA

Maybe I should work awhile. (*Gestures to a desk and stacks of student papers*)

PAUL

The one thing children have to do is *wait*.

LENA

(*Thinks, smiles, begins to gather books*) You may still
have a lot to learn about children.

PAUL

(*Nods*) I'm ready.

When LENA *is ready, she walks past* PAUL *and stops in
front of* LOGAN.

LENA

I'm sorry—

LOGAN

Did you know her?

LENA

(*Shakes her head, waits*) You any kind of farmer?

LOGAN

I worked Mother's garden.

LENA

She like strawberries?

LOGAN

No. She had them for us though—my father and me.

LENA

Then maybe you're my rescue. I've had berry plants for two weeks now, hoping some wise hand would come help me set them.

LOGAN

(*Guarded*) Just in sun—full sun, if you've got it.

LENA

(*Searches his eyes, then nods*) We've got it.

LENA *leaves, not looking back to* PAUL.

LOGAN *shrugs, still puzzled, but follows her.*

PAUL *turns out the light as he leaves last.*

They walk in Indian file up the empty hall, past plaster casts of the Venus de Milo and the Winged Victory.

11

Half an hour later, the porch of LENA'S *house.* PAUL *is seated in a rocker.* LOGAN *stands at the bottom of the steps in the yard, looking toward the road.*

LENA *enters from within through the front screen-door with a tray of Coca-Colas and glasses.*

PAUL *takes one bottle (no glass).*

LENA *looks toward* LOGAN'S *back.*

LOGAN *does not turn.*

                    PAUL
Son—

                    LOGAN
Sir?

                    PAUL
Sit down and drink this dope—cool and soothing.

LOGAN *stays in place.* So LENA *takes two steps forward to serve him.*

PAUL

(*Stops her with a gesture, then stronger to* LOGAN)
You've got the whole rest of your life to stand up in.
(*Points to an empty rocker beside him*)

LOGAN

(*Thinks a moment, looking straight at* PAUL) That may just be another month at most.

PAUL

(*Smiles*) Or another five seconds, for all three of us—this *tree* could fall and mash us to jellybeans.

PAUL *takes a second bottle from* LENA's *tray and extends it toward* LOGAN.

LOGAN *looks up at the bare tree above them. His self-absorption and vague unease at* LENA's *presence are yielding now to innate good-nature and courtesy. He climbs the steps and accepts the bottle.*

LOGAN

(*To* LENA) Thank you, Mrs. Brock.

LENA

Very welcome, Lieutenant.

A car has stopped in front of the house. A girl steps out and thanks the driver.

The three on the porch all watch in silence as GAIL BROCK *comes toward them through the yard, schoolbooks in her arms. She is fifteen; her all-but womanly face still wears a child's serenity.*

LOGAN *is clearly impressed by her beauty and watches her closely.*

At the foot of the steps, GAIL *pauses gravely, looking at* LENA.

LENA

Big day?

GAIL *shakes her head No. She has not looked to* LOGAN, *and the effort to avoid him is barely visible.*

PAUL

You got your hair cut.

GAIL

(*Nodding and touching the ends of her hair*) My friend Becky did it. I think she messed it up.

LOGAN

Not at all.

LENA

Gail, this is Lieutenant Logan Melton.

GAIL

(*Facing him*) Hey. (*Climbs the steps, passes them, and opens the screen door*)

LENA

You promised you'd help me plant strawberries.

GAIL *winces but nods and enters the house.*

LENA

(*To* LOGAN) Where are you stationed now?

LOGAN

Idaho. I'll be shipping out soon—I'm not supposed to say so.

LENA

I won't tell a soul.

LOGAN

Not a *Japanese* soul. (*Loosens his tie, pulls it off, unbuttons his collar*)

PAUL

There's a minimum of them in rural Carolina.

LENA

I'll just go check on Gail—

LOGAN

Can I help her?

LENA

(*Grins*) She's changing into work clothes. She'll manage O.K.

LOGAN

With the planting, I mean—you mentioned strawberries.
(*Looks to* PAUL) We pausing here awhile?

PAUL

(*Nods*) A while.

LOGAN

We could do it—Gail and I. It wouldn't take long.

LENA

Then I'm sure she'd welcome help. (*Waits, then half-whispers to* LOGAN) She'd be too proud to ask, but she's always hoped to meet you.

12

Twenty minutes later, four-thirty p.m. GAIL *and* LOGAN *are squatting in a garden behind the house, planting strawberries with rusty trowels.* GAIL *wears a simple housedress.* LOGAN *wears his undershirt and the trousers of his uniform.* LOGAN *faces* GAIL, *who works intently. They are silent at first.*

GAIL

(*Not looking up*) Don't let Remus bite you.

LOGAN

Who?

GAIL

The snake that lives here. Black as old Uncle Remus.

LOGAN

Too early for snakes. Anyhow, a black snake's the least of my worries.

They work another long silent moment. Then LOGAN
looks to GAIL. *His strong response to her open beauty is
hindered by thoughts of his likely future.*

GAIL

What would be the *most* of your worries?

LOGAN

(*Thinks*) —Ending the war.

GAIL

You'll have a lot of help. You're not the only soldier.

LOGAN *pauses, then laughs.*

GAIL

(*Looking up*) Are you?

LOGAN

No, there's several million more. They kill us one at a
time, just the same.

GAIL

(*Pauses, looking round toward the distant woods*) Seems
pretty safe to me.

LOGAN

I'll be leaving here. (*In all that follows, his vulnerability
to* GAIL'S *magnetism is shown in small helpless gestures
of attraction—any move that will bring his hands nearer
to her*)

GAIL

That wouldn't worry *me*.

LOGAN

You been here all your life?

GAIL

More than fourteen years. We moved here right after my father died—I was six months old. My mother had to work, and she only knew music, so she got a job here. They're crazy for music. (*Waits*) I wish it could have been in a lot bigger place.

LOGAN

(*Looks round*) Seems big enough here—plenty air, plenty trees.

GAIL

(*Smiles*) Trees mostly don't talk.

LOGAN

What you want to talk about?

GAIL

Just *talk*, to hear myself. Mother's always too tired. Everybody else is children.

LOGAN

Dive in. I'm grown and I'm not a bit tired.

GAIL

How old are you?

LOGAN

Twenty.

GAIL

(*Kneels in the row of plants and faces* LOGAN) Does it
ever get better?

LOGAN

(*Kneeling also*) What?

GAIL

I don't know—*life.*

LOGAN

What's wrong with life?

GAIL

(*Thinks*) Oh, it's *taking* too long.

LOGAN

(*Laughs*) What you want it to do?

GAIL

Make me grown-up—soon.

LOGAN

(*Studies her a moment*) You're what?—fifteen? You're
moving right along.

GAIL

(*Unselfconsciously runs a hand across her breasts, half-
whispering*) Claudia Spencer, one grade ahead of me, is
pretty sure she's pregnant.

LOGAN

That's life—speeding up. Where'd she find a father? All boys are in the army.

GAIL

That's what *you* think. We've got plenty boys. I wish they'd draft them sooner.

LOGAN

Don't wish that on anybody, Gail.

GAIL

It's doing *you* good.

LOGAN

(*Laughs*) How's that?

GAIL

You've grown on up. You look a lot better.

LOGAN

Thank you, I guess. But where've you seen me?

GAIL

(*Points quickly to the house*) Your father—pictures of you—he's shown us your pictures long as I remember.

LOGAN

Have you known him that long?

GAIL

(*Nods*) Longer.

LOGAN

(*Mildly curious*) He's worked with your mother.

GAIL

(*Nods, returns to planting*) We heard about *your* mother.

LOGAN

How well did you know her?

GAIL

We never saw her.

LOGAN's *initial sense, in the schoolroom, of something strange begins to deepen now.*

But GAIL, *still planting, forestalls him innocently.*

GAIL

You haven't even planted enough to earn your supper.

LOGAN

(*Returning to work*) Are we eating here?

GAIL

(*Nods*) Are you married?

LOGAN

I thought you knew about me.

GAIL

Not much—just your face.

LOGAN

No ma'm. I'm single. I'll wait to get free. Then I have to finish college.

GAIL

Are you lonesome?

LOGAN

(*Laughs and stops again, facing* GAIL) Not now—not this minute.

GAIL *looks up, smiles quickly but points him to work again. Soon she turns her back and moves away to another row. When she's worked there a moment, she speaks without looking.*

GAIL

If second cousins marry each other, what happens?

LOGAN

(*Laughs*) Beg your pardon?

GAIL

You know—do they have two-headed babies?

LOGAN

I haven't tried it yet. But there's no big shortage of strangers to love.

GAIL

In the army?

LOGAN

—Army *towns*. And in the whole world.

GAIL

(*Thinks*) That's why I want to get out of this place.

LOGAN

You in love with your cousin?

GAIL *turns back to study him carefully, her face entirely neutral.*

GAIL

I could probably love you.

LOGAN

(*Touched, almost shaken*) Not now. I may not last.

GAIL

We're just second cousins—maybe even third.

LOGAN

(*Puzzled but still in the grip of her offer*) We're no kin at all, to the best of my knowledge.

GAIL *shakes her head No.*

LOGAN *slowly stands.*

GAIL *stays in place, a plant in her hand.*

He begins to move toward her.

When he's four steps away, GAIL *looks back quickly to the distant house—no one in sight. Then she rises to meet him.*

LOGAN's *hands stay down; but he pauses a moment, looking past her (though not to the house). Then he leans to kiss the crown of her head.*

GAIL *accepts that, unmoving.* LOGAN *takes a step backward.*

GAIL *studies him, then closes the gap, and cranes up to meet his lips—long but cool. His hands have stayed down.*

GAIL *steps back and bends to collect her trowel.*

LOGAN *does the same.*

They rise together.

GAIL

What happens if cousins *kiss*?

LOGAN

Big babies in loud colors—red, green, orange—that come out talking and can sing on-key.

GAIL

(*Thinks, then sings softly*) Over hill, over dale,
We have hit the dusty trail,
And those caissons go rolling along.

In and out, hear them shout,
"Counter-march and right about,"
And those caissons go rolling along.

She has hit upon the song of the Field Artillery, and
LOGAN *shows some initial resistance; but as she nears the*
end of the verse and moves toward the house, he falls in
beside her and joins the chorus.

LOGAN AND GAIL

Then it's hi! hi! hee! in the field artillery,
Sound off your numbers loud and strong—One! Two!
Wher'er you go, you will always know
That those caissons are rolling along.
Keep them rolling!
And those caissons go rolling along.

13

Two minutes later, nearly five o'clock, the kitchen of the house. LENA *is working at the sink.* PAUL *has removed his tie and is sitting at the central table, calmly reading a magazine. Soft music comes from a big old radio in a corner and continues throughout. The sense is one of accustomed ease.*

Laughter from the backporch steps, climbing feet. GAIL *enters briskly with* LOGAN *behind her, a little abashed.*

PAUL
Sounded like manoeuvres out there. Did you finish?

GAIL *nods and goes to the sink to wash her hands.* LOGAN *brushes his hands together, dusting them off.*

LOGAN
(*To* LENA) They should do all right—course you'll have to wait for berries.

LENA
Thank you, Logan. Thank you very much.

PAUL

She can *not* wait. She's made a walnut pie.

GAIL

I hate black walnuts.

LENA

Then that makes you special.

PAUL

I'm normal. I eat them every chance I get. Logan eats them in his sleep.

LOGAN

(*Confused by the air of ease, to* PAUL) Are you eating here?

PAUL *frowns at the rudeness.*

GAIL *has watched from the sink. She nods to* LOGAN *gravely.*

LENA *faces* LOGAN.

LENA

You'd both be welcome, Logan, to what we've got.

LOGAN *balks a moment, looks to* GAIL's *back (she is still unsmiling), then again to* PAUL.

PAUL *is silent and blank.*

GAIL

Guess what we haven't got?

All face her, relieved.

PAUL

What?

GAIL

Whipping cream.

LENA *rushes to the refrigerator and looks.*

LENA

How did you know that?

GAIL

(*Still not turning*) I *know* things, Mother (*Turns quickly to* LOGAN) I can't eat walnut pie without whipped cream.

PAUL

(*Standing, to* GAIL) Then guide me to cream. We'll go buy some cream.

LENA

(*Glancing at the clock*) But hurry—just a pint—and smell it for onions.

GAIL *dries her hands to go.*

LOGAN *still stands, confused—is he going with them?*

PAUL

You stay here, Son. Try to help out.

LENA

(*To* LOGAN) I'll manage. Get some air.

PAUL

He's had air today and plenty more to come. (*To* LOGAN)
Rest here. Ten minutes. Go count Lena's chickens.

GAIL *is already out of the room.* PAUL *follows to the door.*

PAUL

What else besides cream?

LENA

That's it.

PAUL

Gas is rationed—

LENA

(*Smiles*) I'm sure.

PAUL

(*Going, to* LOGAN) Count the chickens. Kill any snake
you see.

The front screendoor slams shut.

LOGAN *is still near the kitchen door, standing abandoned
and awkward now.*

LENA *returns to work at the sink.*

LENA

There aren't any chickens, Logan. Rest yourself.

LOGAN

(*Moving toward a chair at the table*) Thank you, ma'm.

LENA

The front room might be a little more peaceful. There *is* a piano. Play me something.

LOGAN

(*Standing behind the chair*) It's all right here, if I won't bother you.

LENA

I'm *easy* not to bother. (*But she works intently*)

LOGAN *sits slowly and holds upright a moment. Then he bends to rest his head on the table, his eyes on* LENA.

In the silence LENA *turns to look.*

LOGAN

I can't remember the last time I rested.

LENA

Rest is one thing we've got.

LOGAN *shuts his eyes and quickly seems asleep.*

LENA *turns back to work.*

The radio produces an up-beat song.

LOGAN's *eyes reopen but his head stays down.*

> LOGAN
>
> Maybe I've been too far for my age. (*Smiles crookedly*)

> LENA
>
> You've seen a lot of places.

> LOGAN
>
> (*Still down*) I've seen a lot of trains—the insides of trains from here to Idaho, the old airplane that brought me home.

> LENA
>
> I'd love to fly.

> LOGAN
>
> No you wouldn't, no ma'm.

> LENA
>
> Not now. After all this mess is over.

> LOGAN
>
> (*Suddenly sits up*) You think it *will* be?

> LENA
>
> Sure—before another Christmas.

> LOGAN
>
> Will I live to see it?

LENA

(*Forced to turn and see him*) Christmas or peace?

LOGAN

I'd take either one.

LENA

You look strong to me.

LOGAN

My mother *looked* strong.

LENA *pauses and then turns back to work.*

LOGAN

What kin are you to her?

LENA

(*Waits*) I never got to see her.

LOGAN

Gail said we were cousins. Mother had a world of cousins—I barely knew five.

LENA

Gail thinks a lot. Remember when you were fifteen years old.

LOGAN

I'm thinking right now.

LENA

(*Looks back quickly, smiling*) You were told to rest.

LOGAN

(*Gentle but firm*) I've been told everything but what I need.

LENA

That's a normal predicament, wouldn't you say?

LOGAN

(*Still gently but strengthening*) What?—have your young mother fall dead on the floor a few days before you're due to ship out to face a billion armed Japanese defending their homes, and me in just *skin*? (*Touches his cheek*)

LENA

(*Calmly*) I said you'd make it.

LOGAN

You said I was strong. I'm not—the world knows it.

LOGAN's *face is suddenly bathed in tears. He stares on at* LENA, *unashamed or desperate.*

In the silence she turns and receives the sight. She stays in place a moment, then dries her hands, steps to the table, and sits facing LOGAN. *Her hands are on the edge but do not reach toward him.*

By now, real pain contorts his tears—the shame of fear and the shame of pent-up grief for his mother.

LENA

(*Half-whispers*) Nobody's here but me, and I don't count. Let it all out, as much as will come.

LOGAN

(*After long silence, shakes his head; then with great difficulty*) This is not for me.

LENA

I think I know that.

LOGAN

(*Still straining*) I loved my mother more than anything else.

LENA

She wanted you to.

LOGAN

I caused her to die.

LENA

You were two thousand miles away.

LOGAN

It worried her to death—me going to war. She had plans for me. They were getting all ruined.

LENA

(*Smiling*) They're not. You look fine to me. You're safe.

LOGAN

I *may* be—I may turn out to be an honorable man with good work to do and strong happy children. She didn't wait to see.

LENA

It was just her time. I *believe* in fate—I've had to. If I didn't, I'd have run wild years ago—the stuff I've seen. (*But she smiles again*)

LOGAN

(*Studies her—the first time*) Who are you?

LENA

(*Waits, gestures round her*) What you see.

LOGAN *looks round as though there were answers to find.*

LOGAN

Why am I here?

LENA

(*Thinks, then laughs and stands*) To try my grand food —I cook much better than I teach children music. You're bound to be hungry.

LOGAN

(*Also stands*) I don't think so—

His grief, fear, and bafflement are at their strongest. He walks to the open kitchen door, steps out, takes the back steps quickly, then runs through the yard toward the garden and the woods.

LENA *pauses, then slowly walks to the door, and sees him vanish in the darkening trees.*

14

Immediately after, five-thirty, PAUL *and* GAIL *are returning in the car, with a small bag of groceries. They ride in easy silence, their faces dazed by private thoughts. At last, almost in sight of* LENA's—

PAUL

Did he measure up?

GAIL

Sir?—to what?

PAUL

Logan—did he meet your expectations?

GAIL

(*Thinks*) I guess so. (*Turns to her window, a stretch of trees*) I'd waited so long, I thought he'd seem older.

PAUL

He's tired today.

GAIL

Of what?

PAUL

This war.

GAIL

I'm tired of the war. It's all I remember—Franklin D. Roosevelt and rationed shoes.

PAUL

You need new shoes?

GAIL

Not really—maybe sandals if summer ever comes.

PAUL

We'll see to that. (*Long pause*) Has your mother been O.K.?

GAIL

(*Still staring aside*) *You* saw her. You've known her much longer.

PAUL

Pardon me.

GAIL

(*Waits a long silence, then faces his profile*) Are *you* all right?

PAUL

(*Smiles*) I haven't checked lately. (*Feels his heart*)
The *clock* is still ticking.

GAIL

Was the funeral nice?

PAUL

(*Thinks, then smiles*) *Nice,* very nice. Even *she'd* have
been pleased. Mostly music. I throttled the minister.

GAIL

Really?

PAUL

I told him any *words* might be hard on Logan, having
come so far and facing his future.

GAIL

(*Waits, then with unexpected fervor*) I love him.

PAUL

Not yet.

GAIL

That's what Logan said. I can disobey you both.

They stare forward at the road in silence.

15

Immediately after. LOÇAN *is walking in a slow intensity, on a path through the woods behind* LENA's *house. Sooner than he expects, he breaks through onto a clearing—a small creek, late sun.*

He turns to follow the water downstream and, round a bend, comes on a ring of stones laid out on the bank— a once-cleared space returning to weeds—ten feet across with a big flat central stone.

He enters, studies the ground, sees something, bends, scratches at it. First he unearths the arm of a small doll. Then he digs on, finds the rest, and lifts it—remains of a doll ten inches long, missing one eye and badly weathered but grinning gamely.

He replaces it, covers it carefully, presses the dirt with his foot.

Then he sits on the central stone and stares up at the sky through branches.

16

Immediately after. LENA *is setting four places at the table in her dining room. She pauses to hear* PAUL'S *car arrive but continues working as* PAUL *and* GAIL *enter.*

GAIL *goes to her own room.*

PAUL *goes to the kitchen, finds it empty.*

PAUL
(*Setting a bag on the counter*)
Anybody home?

LENA
(*Long pause*) No.

PAUL *follows her voice, finds her standing on the far side of the dining table—finished and facing him.*

PAUL
You are, plain as day.

LENA

But you said *home*. Whose home is this?

PAUL *winces slightly, then shakes his head—she is talking too openly, too soon.*

LENA

(*Calm*) He's gone.

PAUL

Logan? Where?

LENA

I don't know—out the back.

PAUL

I didn't think you'd tell him.

LENA

You did, Paul—you know it. You hoped you could leave here to buy a pint of cream and come back ten minutes later—all fixed, seventeen years dissolved: one big *family*, happy as frogs.

PAUL

Are frogs happy?—no, maybe you're right. Sure I wanted no pain for everybody here. Wouldn't that be normal?—they're all I've got.

LENA

(*Thinks, nods*) That would be normal—for you, Paul. For you.

She walks directly past him toward the kitchen.

PAUL *stands a moment, then steps to the neat table, strokes a bare plate with his fingers. Then he follows* LENA.

But the kitchen is empty again.

PAUL

Lena?

LENA

(*Long pause*) I'm on the back steps.

PAUL

(*Looking to the pantry*) You want a short drink?

LENA

No, I don't.

PAUL *goes to the pantry, finds the fifth of bourbon behind rows of food, returns to the sink, pours himself four ounces straight, and knocks it back in one long swallow. He shudders hard, then turns toward the front of the house.*

PAUL

Gail?

GAIL

(*Distant, muffled*) What?

PAUL

Don't call me *what*. Where are you?

GAIL

Getting dressed.

PAUL

You were already dressed.

GAIL

I'll be there in a minute.

PAUL

(*Looking toward* LENA) Take your time. We're dying, is all—slow starvation.

He pours another drink (two ounces) and swallows.

Then he goes to LENA; *stands a moment, looking out toward the dimming woods, and sits two steps above her.*

PAUL

You given up cooking?

LENA

(*Not turning*) It's in the oven, ready whenever you are.

PAUL

I'm ready. Gail's beautifying herself for Logan. He'll be back soon.

LENA

What makes you think so?

PAUL

I've known him all his life.

LENA

He hasn't known you.

PAUL

Well, you seem to have helped him. He'll be in soon.

LENA

I can teach little children to halfway sing. I don't offer courses in the mysteries of God.

PAUL

(*Smiling*) Am I one of those?

LENA

You're right up there with earthquakes, glaciers—trench-mouth. (*Turns back to face him, almost smiles*) I didn't tell Logan a thing, Paul—really. That's your choice to make. Gail seems to have told him they were some kind of cousins, her and him.

PAUL

She's fallen for him.

LENA

(*Looking outward again*) I did too, seventeen years ago.

PAUL

He was three years old. You didn't *know* about him.

LENA

I met you—I knew you—he's almost the image of you
at that age, every way *I* can see.

PAUL

He's nicer than me—he pays more attention. So he has
more worries. When I met you I didn't have a care to
my name. (*Lays both hands on* LENA's *shoulders*)

LENA

(*Looking outward*) The whole Depression was one year
away. You had a wife that you said barely noticed you.

PAUL

Don't blame her now. She was tending Logan. I doubt
a woman ever loved a child more than she loved Logan
back then. I was just a trusty friend that showed up for
weekends.

LENA

(*His hands on her still, still looking out*) I haven't told
Logan a single secret, Paul.

PAUL

What drove him off then?

LENA

We mentioned his mother—and the war—and her wor-
rying. He *knows* she died of dread for him. So now he
plans to die just to even the score.

PAUL

(*Takes his hands back*) He very well might.

LENA *turns half-around and studies* PAUL *a moment.*

He waits, then nods.

LENA

Then go find him now.

PAUL

And tell him what?

LENA

(*Thinks*) —That he's welcome here. Anything else you want, just no more lies.

PAUL *thinks, nods, studies* LENA. *Then he bends to kiss her.*

*She accepts him calmly. The sound of steps behind them. They continue close—*PAUL's *chin on the crown of* LENA's *hair, both looking to the woods.*

GAIL *is just above them, dressed and combed. She takes the sight of the adults in stride.*

GAIL

Where's Logan?

PAUL

On a hike.

GAIL

Does he have to practice?

PAUL

Oh yes. They give you leave, but you got to practice.

LENA

(*Points*) He's down by the creek, I guess. He *headed* there.

GAIL

Is he coming in to eat?

PAUL

I'll go get him.

GAIL

Let me.

PAUL

(*Rising*) Help your mother.

GAIL

I know the woods best.

PAUL

(*Facing her firmly*) No. I said I was going and I am. I'll find him. You wait.

PAUL *descends the steps and moves through the yard, pausing to check a parked lawnmower.*

Dusky light. LENA *sits on.*

GAIL *slowly sits in* PAUL's *place. They face the woods, silent.*

17

Six o'clock. PAUL *reaches the bank of the creek without calling. He pauses there a moment, and stares upstream. The light is dimmer. He turns downstream and, every few steps, calls at normal volume—*

PAUL

Logan—

No answer. As PAUL *flanks the abandoned ring of stones, he fails to see* LOGAN, *who is lying on his back with his head on the central stone, his feet toward* PAUL.

LOGAN's *eyes are barely open and register no recognition of his father.*

When PAUL *has walked well past and called again,* LOGAN *answers.*

LOGAN

(*Still supine*) He's here.

PAUL *walks toward the voice but takes awhile to find him. At last, in the entrance to the ring,* PAUL *stops.*

PAUL
How is he?

LOGAN
Haven't asked him lately.

PAUL
(*Enters and sits on a flat stone*) He'd better check soon. This ground looks damp. (*Lays his palm on the ground*) He'll be rusting-out fast.

LOGAN
Good.

PAUL
(*Waits*) Sit up, Son. I've lost enough friends.

LOGAN *slowly pulls up, then sits on the stone he has leaned against. The doll he discovered is now at his feet. He bends to touch it.*

PAUL
Where'd you rescue that?

LOGAN
In here. It was buried.

PAUL
(*Bends to look*) Some old friend of Gail's.

LOGAN

What is this place?

PAUL

A creek-bank. Some woods.

LOGAN

You could answer me. I'm harmless now.

PAUL

(*Smiles*) When were you harmful?

LOGAN

Till the day Mother died—I could tell on you.

PAUL

What did you know?

LOGAN

Absolutely nothing.

PAUL

What did you think?

LOGAN

(*Lifts the doll to his knees*) —That you were several people.

PAUL

Did you like any of them?

LOGAN

The happy one, I told you.

PAUL

(*Waits*) Thank you. He's still alive, I guess—not as young as he was.

LOGAN

But *happy*, right?

PAUL

I will be again, I trust. We've just had a funeral.

LOGAN

(*Calmly*) And you may have another one. How would *that* leave you?

PAUL

A good deal sadder. Your mother had a life; you haven't had yours.

LOGAN

Lena Brock says I'll have it. (*Faces* PAUL) While you were at the store, she promised me I'd make it.

PAUL

Then you will. She's *smart*.

LOGAN

Who is she?

PAUL

You've seen her—a grade-school teacher with a daughter to raise.

LOGAN

The daughter says we're kin. Gail told me she's my cousin.

PAUL

She's not.

LOGAN

What is she then? What is all this here?

PAUL *waits, then rises and moves to the old doll lying on the ground. He lifts it by a leg and takes it with him back to his seat. He holds it out before him, studying it.*

PAUL

This is a doll I gave Gail Brock for Christmas when she was maybe four years old. (*Touches the doll's empty eyesocket*) When it went half-blind, we buried it here and got a new one—a whole string of new ones down through the years till just the other day, seems like, she outgrew them.

PAUL *rises again and this time returns the doll to its grave. He covers it carefully with dirt, then sits.*

LOGAN

Is that my answer?

PAUL

(*Waits, then smiles*) *Ought* to be—smart as you are.

LOGAN

She's your daughter.

PAUL

I'm her father.

LOGAN

What's Lena?

PAUL

Her mother—all you saw was true. I never lied to you.

LOGAN

You recall *I* had a mother. How much truth did she see?

PAUL

Don't you think that was her and my business, Son?

LOGAN

Yes sir, I do—long as she was alive to watch it and suffer. But now you've landed me in it, face down.

PAUL

Your mother never watched one second of this, never knew it was here.

LOGAN

She's bound to have felt it. She hardly *had* skin.

PAUL

Did she tell you she did?

LOGAN

She very seldom told me things about you.

PAUL

And she told you everything she felt—*you* were what she felt.

LOGAN

Then why have *you* told me—and now, of all times?

PAUL

I always wanted to tell you somehow. When you'd run out to meet me on Friday evening, it was all I could do not to tell you right then. I wanted you to watch both halves of my contentment and share it if you could. I still do now. You're a full strong man. When I'm gone, you'll need to know.

LOGAN

You're trusting I'll outlast you.

PAUL

You said Lena promised you. Lena's hardly ever wrong.

The light is scarce now. LOGAN *stands and walks to the doll's covered grave. With one foot he slowly but firmly packs the dirt. Then he looks to* PAUL *and holds his arms out loosely at his sides—a shrug of dazed bafflement.*

PAUL

Supper's ready, if you are.

> LOGAN

What if I'm not?

> PAUL

It's ready all the same. We'd eat it without you—wouldn't relish it much.

> LOGAN

I doubt I know enough to walk in there again.

> PAUL

I'll tell it all there. I can tell it truer there.

> LOGAN

What does Gail know?

> PAUL

The bare-bone facts—Lena told her two years ago.

> LOGAN

That didn't set her back?

> PAUL

Considerably, at first. She wouldn't speak to me for two weeks running, till she saw she didn't have much of a choice—it was speak or go dumb to one of the two things on earth that loved her.

> LOGAN

(*Nods*) She's looking elsewhere.

> PAUL

For what?

LOGAN

Things to love her—more men than you.

PAUL

(*Thinks, then rises*) She'll find them.

LOGAN

She told me we were cousins.

PAUL

She used to believe that. She was sounding you out.

LOGAN

I kissed her.

PAUL

That was typical, at least.

LOGAN

(*Half-smiles*) Of what?

PAUL

—The *block*. (*Taps his own chest*) The block you're
chipped from, like it or not.

PAUL *gestures for* LOGAN *to precede him out.*

LOGAN *stays in place.*

LOGAN

I may not like it.

PAUL

I'm what you've got.

LOGAN

I may not want you. (*Walks to the back of the circle and looks toward the house, hid by trees*) I can hitch out of here now, clean as a whistle, and be back in Idaho and never *see* you.

PAUL

I hope you won't.

LOGAN

Why?—to save your face with this other crowd? (*Points toward* LENA'S)

PAUL

Not much of a crowd—less if *you* go.

LOGAN *steps outside the stones that edge the ring and moves toward the woods—pathless, nearly dark.*

PAUL

I can tell you why.

LOGAN *crashes out of sight through the thicket.*

PAUL

(*Louder*) Show a little mercy—you die, it'll kill me.

Silence from LOGAN, *then a slow crackle in the leaves as he turns. He comes back as far as the edge of the ring and stands, obscured.*

LOGAN

You may have earned that.

PAUL *takes two steps toward him.*

LOGAN *takes a step back.*

PAUL

(*Hotly*) Who are you to judge me?

LOGAN

Something you made, that's watched you closely for twenty years now—all you'd let me see. (*Comes two steps forward, his foot on a stone at the edge of the ring*) I dreamed up whole happy lives for you but nothing like this—a small-time cheat.

PAUL, *for years, has dreaded hearing that. It hits him now like a great body-blow. He rides out the first pain, then goes back and sits in his former place.*

PAUL

May I speak to that? Then do what you have to.

LOGAN *waits, nods once, but stays in place.*

PAUL

I can't talk to somebody staring *down* on me.

Slowly LOGAN *steps back into the ring but sits on the edge. He faces* PAUL *blankly.*

PAUL

(*Thinks*) A *cheat*? Well, O.K. if it makes you feel lighter. But aside from what I told your mother in our wedding vows—and God in Heaven knows *they* can't be kept—I never broke a promise to cherish her.

LOGAN

(*Points toward* LENA's) This is *cherishing*?

PAUL

(*Thinks, nods*) *Yes.* I'm coming to that. But I asked to be heard—listen please or leave.

LOGAN *bends and traces lines in the dirt.*

PAUL

—A *cheat*: sure, take it. But small-time, no. I may not be the world's best music-salesman—though I think I've brought pleasure to a good many homes—but what you can't see is big, Logan, *big.* (*Taps his chest again and goes on with real intensity, though with a salesman's practiced fluency and speed*) I've got a lot in here—or they *put* a lot in; it's not my fault. Your mother was a kind intelligent person, and I loved her every day of her life that I knew her. But, Son, she couldn't handle *half* of me.

LOGAN *raises a hand to stop his father.*

PAUL *nods but continues.*

PAUL

Before you were born, I'd begun to know that your mother needed much less from life than me. She could sit in a room and watch daylight spread across a plaster wall, millimeters at a time (*Shakes his head in wonder*) and be calm as a leaf. *Saints* do the same thing.

LOGAN *can nod now, yielding slightly.*

PAUL

Anyhow, she gave me what she had to give—three days of me a week was plenty for her; she could brace herself for that—and here you came.

LOGAN

—The accident.

PAUL

Not at all. I planned you as carefully as the Normandy invasion. I thought you'd bring her on into the world, get some fresh blood moving my way through her veins—

LOGAN

But she just watched me like daylight on the wall.

PAUL

(*Thinks, smiles*) Of course, she didn't have to change diapers on daylight—she *worked* on you.

LOGAN

You'd brought her to life.

PAUL

(*Thinks*) Yes—for you.

LOGAN

Did you blame me for it?

PAUL

(*Firmly*) Never. Not once.

LOGAN

You'd already found Lena.

PAUL

Not for three years, no—more than one thousand days: lying round country towns in hot rented rooms, hoping some soul would scrape up the money and want a piano. And I didn't *find* Lena, didn't hunt her down. She was just there one day.

LOGAN

Needing a piano—

PAUL

I started that in her, the music part. She was teaching geometry—right out of school herself—and rooming in a house where I used to stay.

LOGAN

Here?

PAUL

Oh no. (*Points*) —In Fulton, deep *down* in the sticks:

some boys in her class had sons of their own. It wasn't till I knew she was pregnant that I moved her. She saw I was married, (*Shows his wedding band*) and I saw it wasn't right in any way except the way I needed—*she could use me up*. Whatever else you think, believe one thing—Lena Brock filled every other hunger I had, that you didn't fill. Back then I could watch her—watch her shape in a room—and feel repaid for everything I'd lost.

LOGAN

When did you marry her?

PAUL

(*A little surprised*) I had a wife, Son—till just the other day.

LOGAN

Who did people think you were?—Lena's family and friends.

PAUL

She'd been raised by an aunt in South Carolina—her parents died young, in the flu epidemic. And once she moved here, she was just a young widow with a baby girl.

LOGAN

(*Persisting*) Who were you though? Who are you now?

PAUL

I've never asked her. She's made her own arrangements.

LOGAN

How can she be happy?

PAUL

I wouldn't ask her that.

LOGAN

—Thanksgiving, Christmas, Easter: you were always with us. She and Gail got—what?—three nights a week?

PAUL

Less most weeks. I've had to do my job.

LOGAN

How could they stand it?

PAUL

They've got a private strength they've managed to store. (*Waits*) They've wanted to know *you*—

LOGAN

Now you'll bring them home.

PAUL

It's *your* home and *mine*.

LOGAN

Will you move here?

PAUL

(*Waits, smiles, then rises*) You always want to be a long-range *prophet*. All I can prophesy from here is supper. We're long-overdue.

PAUL *bows slightly at the waist and gestures with a hand toward the exit from the ring.*

LOGAN *stays in place, seated, facing his father. His last question survives on his face.*

PAUL *steps toward him, stops an arm's length away.*

PAUL
You're not the only thing here that has to die, Son. Chances are, you'll outlast me by years—me and half of these trees. (*Gestures overhead*) Don't store up memories too hard to bear. (*Extends his right hand and tentatively smiles*) Bless me old prophet.

PAUL *extends his right hand.*

LOGAN *studies it a moment, then clasps it with his left hand and accepts a pull upward.*

LOGAN
What do I say—in there—if I go?

PAUL
Everything your mother taught you—kind courtesy, at least.

LOGAN *faces his father, two feet away. He searches* PAUL's *face and gives no response; but when* PAUL *breaks the gaze and turns to leave,* LOGAN *follows him out. They walk past the creek and into the dark still woods in silence.*

18

Five minutes later, LENA's *backyard.* PAUL *moves first from darkness into the porchlight's glow. He stops at the foot of the steps and waits for* LOGAN.

LOGAN *stops three paces back. The sound of a piano comes from the house—an adequate performance of Chopin's Prelude in D Flat (the "Raindrop").*

LOGAN
Which one is that? (*Nods his head toward the house*)

PAUL
Gail, I guess—she picks the heavy stuff.

LOGAN
Why not call her my sister?

PAUL
(*Thinks, unsmiling*) That's your choice to make.

LOGAN
I haven't made it yet.

PAUL

(*Half-smiles*) What you call *me* now?

LOGAN

(*Waits*) Big Mystery of the Ages—

PAUL

(*Laughs*) I hope Time has got something bigger to unfold.

LOGAN

(*Nods*) You mentioned eating supper. That'll do for a start.

PAUL *nods, turns, climbs the steps with* LOGAN *close behind. The Chopin is ending.*

19

LENA's *dining room, seven o'clock.* LENA *is seated at one end of the table,* PAUL *at the other.* LOGAN *and* PAUL *face one another from the two sides. They have finished the main course, and* GAIL *has gone to the kitchen to fetch the walnut pie.*

LOGAN

(*To* LENA) Were there any Russian triumphs?

LENA

(*Smiles, puzzled*) Beg your pardon?

LOGAN

You told your class to listen to the news.

LENA

Lord, I forgot.

GAIL

(*From the kitchen, whipping cream*) I didn't. We've captured most of Iwo Jima now.

PAUL

How was Mrs. Roosevelt's day?

LENA

She seems to be standing still for a change. (*Smiles*)
Tired as me.

PAUL

She won't rest long. (*To* LOGAN) You get to Japan, she'll
be there to meet you—Eleanor with fresh hot doughnuts
on the beach.

The joke falls flat. LENA *glances to* LOGAN.

LOGAN *traces deep lines with a fingernail in the table-cloth.*

GAIL *appears in the door with the pie and a bowl of
whipped cream.*

LENA

Here's some fresh cream for now.

GAIL *sets it before her, while* LENA *brings plates from the
sideboard.*

GAIL *sits and* LENA, *standing, carefully serves the splendid
pie.*

LOGAN *gets the first plate.*

LOGAN

Thank you both.

GAIL

Thank yourself. You earned it.

LOGAN *waits while all the others are served. He is still but not calm—consciously subdued.*

LENA *sets the remains of the pie on the sideboard and takes her chair again. As she lifts her fork—*

LENA

This will have to stand-in for champagne. (*Takes a small piece of pie on her fork, holds it out*) —Logan's safe and certain return home soon.

GAIL *and* PAUL *follow suit.*

LOGAN *watches* GAIL *gravely.*

GAIL

(*Suddenly fervent*) Let this be your home now.

PAUL *glances to* LENA.

LENA *shows no response but looks to* LOGAN.

LOGAN *takes a slow bite of pie.*

LOGAN

(*To* GAIL) You don't know me yet. I'm no sort of hero, in war or peace. (*Thinks, then to* LENA) My mother had me planned as the first big Protestant piano genius with short *combed* hair. (*To* PAUL) I didn't have the patience to work alone. (*To* GAIL *again*) But thank you still.

GAIL
We don't have to *know* you. I told you we'd been looking at pictures of you ever since I remember.

LOGAN *eats another bite.*

PAUL *and* LENA *are eating watchfully.*

LOGAN
(*To Gail*) I regret you had to put up with that. (*Turns to* LENA) You too, Mrs. Brock.

GAIL *looks to* LENA, *then back to* LOGAN.

GAIL
We liked it. Tell him, Mother.

LENA *looks to* PAUL.

PAUL *nods.*

LENA *sets down her fork and turns to* LOGAN, *unsmiling.*

LENA
We knew your face from the time you *had* a face. Your father would show us your pictures twice a year—the ones he'd take at Christmas, the ones from summer. Gail's got a picture of you framed on her dresser—the day you

were commissioned. (*Looks to* PAUL) Here he is and you were right.

GAIL

(*To* LOGAN) Now you'll get *stuck-up*.

PAUL

Let him. He deserves it.

LOGAN

(*To* LENA) I'm sorry.

LENA *nods a dignified acceptance, a little surprised to find she has needed the apology for years.*

GAIL

For what?

They all look to GAIL *but no one answers.*

GAIL

(*To* LENA) I liked it—didn't you?

PAUL

(*To* GAIL) *She* told him. Eat your pie.

GAIL

I'm sick of pie.

PAUL

(*Smiles*) The poor little Chinese children would love it.

GAIL

Then mail it to them. (*Pushes the plate in* PAUL'*s direction*)

LENA

I may let you take it to them—on foot through the water —if you don't cheer up.

GAIL

Gladly. Any place would be better.

GAIL *slumps in a sulk.*

PAUL *is amused.* LENA *is embarrassed.*

LOGAN *has finished his first slice of pie.*

LOGAN

(*Reaching out*) I'm pitiful enough. Can I finish it for you?

GAIL *nods, still fuming, and* LOGAN *takes her plate.*

LENA

You may get *rabies,* LOGAN.

LOGAN

I've had the shots—*one* thing the army's good for.

LOGAN *tries to eat comically—elaborate chewing.*

GAIL *watches, unamused.*

LOGAN

Found an old buddy of yours in the woods.

GAIL

(*Reluctant*) I don't have buddies.

PAUL

He found one anyhow.

GAIL

(*To* LOGAN) Who?

LOGAN

(*Still eating*) Long-lost and miserable.

PAUL

Neglected and crippled.

LOGAN

Left for dead.

PAUL

Least she's out of her pain.

GAIL *is torn now between her prior sulk, her present curiosity, and the fear of being tricked.*

GAIL

I've never hurt anybody bad as that. (*Looks to* LENA)

LENA

(*Raises hands in bafflement*) Not so far as I know. Of course, you're grown now. There's a lot I don't see.

PAUL

This was the worst.

GAIL *is suddenly in tears—no sound, real pain.*

*All watch her a moment, surprised by their power to
ruin her pleasure, but no one moves.*

GAIL *faces* LOGAN, *still silent but asking relief from him.*

LOGAN *stands in place.*

20

A quarter-hour later in the dark woods beside the creek. LOGAN *walks with a flashlight held before him.* GAIL *follows closely.*

LOGAN *turns into the ring, lays the light on the central stone (shining at the ground), kneels at the grave, and digs with gentle hands. When he's found the doll again, he brushes at her face and holds her out to* GAIL.

GAIL *is reluctant but finally takes her by the leg, in one hand.*

LOGAN

Remember now?

GAIL

Maybe so. There's a lot I forget.

LOGAN

Dad said you and he left it here when it broke.

He quickly smooths the dirt, then stands.

GAIL

He was always bringing me dolls—dolls, dolls. They were meant to make me like him.

LOGAN

Did they work?

GAIL

(*Studies the doll's face*) No. (*Touches the ruined eye*) I liked him anyway. We didn't get a whole lot of people through here—still don't, I told you. I like everybody I possibly can.

LOGAN *smiles and steps back to sit on the center stone.*

GAIL

Let's don't stay here please.

LOGAN

Got homework to do?

GAIL

(*Nods*) Latin—but that's not why.

LOGAN

(*Smiles*) Scared of Nazi bombers?

GAIL

(*Laughs*) I *used* to be. When the war first started, I thought every plane passing over at night had me in the bombsight. Now I doubt even *Germans* would want this place.

LOGAN

Seems nice to me.

GAIL

It's better right down by the creek.

LOGAN

I could build a fire here—

GAIL

(*Suddenly firm*) I said I couldn't stay here.

LOGAN

(*Shrugs, gestures*) Lead the way, lady.

GAIL

Don't make fun. This is where I was miserable.

LOGAN

What happened here?

GAIL *pauses, then turns and walks from the ring. In three steps she's vanished.*

LOGAN *turns on the flashlight. The doll lies skewed at his feet, dropped by* GAIL. *He stands, leaving it, and follows* GAIL.

She is kneeling on the creekbank, her right hand in the water.

LOGAN *moves up beside her and stands four feet away.*

LOGAN

Is it cold?

GAIL

No, warm for some reason. You can sit down here.

LOGAN

Thank you. I'm tired. (*Puts a hand in the water, pulls it back quickly*) Gail, it's cold as *glaciers*!

GAIL

I knew you wouldn't like it.

LOGAN

(*Laughs*) I just told a simple truth. (*Blows on his hand to warm it*)

GAIL

I used to love it here.

LOGAN

You said you were miserable.

GAIL

That's *why* I loved it. I came here and talked to what   ·
couldn't talk back—rocks, leaves, lizards, frogs.

LOGAN

What would you say?

GAIL

I'd ask for things—a life like everybody else: some sisters maybe.

LOGAN

Wouldn't God be the one to ask? Do lizards answer prayer?

GAIL

In stories, sure. No, we don't go to church; so God's not something I think much about.

LOGAN

Everybody else is—praying for peace. Stuff like that.

GAIL

God made lizards. They can carry the message.

LOGAN

They never do seem to have got you the *sisters*.

GAIL

Too late now.

LOGAN

Why?

GAIL

(*Searches his face*) Boy, where have you been?

LOGAN

All over—here to Idaho.

GAIL

I got you instead.

LOGAN

(*Lost*) Ma'm?

GAIL

You—not a sister.

LOGAN

(*Smiles*) Thank you, ma'm.

GAIL

Stuck-up—

LOGAN

O.K. then, I'm sorry.

GAIL

(*Searches him again and leans a little closer*) *I'm* not—any more.

She slowly leans farther.

LOGAN *waits in place.*

She brushes her lips against his, then retreats.

LOGAN

(*Touching his mouth*) You know I'm not your cousin?

GAIL

I know what they *told* me. (*Points toward the house*)

LOGAN

Do you think they've told us the whole truth now?

GAIL

I don't much care, do you?

LOGAN *thinks, then reaches a hand toward her face. His thumb strokes her brow, smoothing the hairs again and again.*

GAIL *accepts it calmly.*

LOGAN

I guess I do—I plan to be a lawyer.

GAIL

People won't blame *you.*

LOGAN

(*Smiles*) I didn't mean that. I'll just need to know plain facts someday. I may have to manage all this if Dad dies.

GAIL

He won't. And forget about *facts*—I've been told more versions of them and who they are than the Bible tells of Moses and the Jews.

LOGAN

By Lena?

GAIL

(*Nods*) —They've known each other from the time they were *children*—they never saw each other till after I was *born*—you used to live with us when I was a *baby*— we're cousins; we're not—we're sister and br—

LOGAN *stops her with a hand to her lips.*

They stay a moment silent. Then they sit back a little from one another.

LOGAN *lies back on the ground.*

LOGAN
(*To the dark trees above*) Let's let the facts wait.

GAIL
For what?

LOGAN
To see if I get back.

GAIL
From where?

LOGAN
Wherever I go tomorrow—home to my mother's old house, then Idaho, then the whole blue Pacific, then God knows where.

GAIL
What if you don't?

LOGAN
Lena said I would.

GAIL

Lena says a lot—she's a *schoolteacher*, Logan. They can talk lawyers down.

LOGAN *takes that in silence, staring up.*

GAIL *moves over, knees almost against his side.*

He reaches blindly for her wrist, lays her hand on the center of his chest. They stay thus, silent. Then—

LOGAN

You've talked *me* down anyhow. You a teacher too?

GAIL

No, I'm a doctor. (*Feels for his heart, then counts the beats*) One—two—three—four. *You're* still alive.

LOGAN

And strong?

GAIL

—As a bear.

LOGAN

But with much better manners.

GAIL

I thought people didn't have to have manners now—the war and all.

LOGAN

Well, *war*-time manners. I try to have those.

GAIL *nods but stays in place, her hand now flat on his heart.*

LOGAN *reaches slowly for the crown of her head and bends that gently toward him.*

GAIL *stops the move eight inches from his lips and searches his eyes.*

GAIL

You sure about this?

LOGAN

No.

GAIL

What if you come back?

LOGAN

Then I'll have to *get* sure. I'll be another man.

GAIL *waits a long moment. Then his hand brings her lightly to rest on his lips—a long still kiss.*

21

A *half-hour later in* LENA's *dark yard, the bottom of the kitchen steps.* GAIL *and* LOGAN *approach, close but not touching. The porchlight is on—and a dim glow from the kitchen—but the house is silent.*

GAIL *takes the lead to climb the steps.*

LOGAN *hooks a finger in the back of her belt, stops and turns her. He studies her face.*

> LOGAN

I'll say goodbye here.

> GAIL

I'll see you at breakfast.

> LOGAN

I guess we'll push on. Dad has to work tomorrow.

> GAIL

The nearest hotel is thirty miles east, and it'll be shut down tight by now. This isn't *Idaho.*

LOGAN

You got room here?

GAIL

I'll sleep with Mother. You and Paul can have my room.

LOGAN

He may not want that.

GAIL

(*Nods*) He will.

LOGAN

I won't sleep a minute—he snores like a walrus.

GAIL

Sleep's a big superstition. Some weeks I don't sleep an hour all-told.

LOGAN

Will you tonight?

GAIL

(*Thinks*) I might have to dream. (*Looks toward the woods*) Have you got an address?

LOGAN

It may change soon.

GAIL

I guess Paul'll know it.

LOGAN

So will you.

GAIL

O.K.

She smiles mildly and turns to go in.

LOGAN

Goodbye though.

GAIL

(*Smiling*) O.K.

She reaches down and touches his forehead lightly. Then she turns and climbs quickly toward the kitchen.

22

Immediately after in LENA's *kitchen. The room is clean of all traces of supper. The only light is from a kerosene lamp on the central table. In its glow* LENA *sits at the table, marking student papers. As* GAIL *and* LOGAN *enter,* LENA *looks up—tired but suppressing anxiety.*

LENA

(*To* GAIL) Which one was it?—Ethel?

GAIL *stops, three steps into the room, baffled by the question.*

LENA

—The poor dead doll. Was it Ethel or Maxine?

GAIL

It must have been Patricia, but she's pretty far gone.

LENA

I trust you reinterred her.

LOGAN

She's all right. She won't feel a thing.

LENA

Miss Gail Brock won't be feeling much either if she doesn't tuck into that Latin homework.

GAIL

Can I work in your room?

LENA

Help yourself—just *work*.

GAIL *nods and moves to leave the room.*

LENA

Tell Logan "Good night."

GAIL

I already did.

Not looking again to LOGAN, *she leaves.*

He smiles to her back as she vanishes in the hall. Then he slowly looks to LENA.

LOGAN

Where's Dad?

LENA

In the living room, snoozing on the world's worst sofa.

LOGAN

Is there some kind of plan about where we spend the night?

LENA

(*Laughs a little*) Nothing under *this* roof was ever planned. But you're welcome here.

LOGAN

Thank you. If he's already out, we'd better just leave him.

LENA

You sleepy?

LOGAN

No ma'm. I'm on Idaho time.

LENA

Would a cup of coffee kill you?

LOGAN

I doubt it.

LENA

Sit down then.

She sweeps the papers to one side, stands, goes to the stove, and pours two cups of coffee.

LOGAN *takes the chair opposite hers.*

She returns, puts the coffee down, and sits again.

LOGAN

(*Points to the oil lamp*) You blow a fuse in here?

LENA

No, I just like to work by oil light. Takes me back to my log-cabin youth. May become the first woman-president this way. (*Sips her coffee*)

LOGAN

You're from South Carolina?

LENA

(*Nods*) I was—back before man invented the wheel. Paul tell you my history?

LOGAN

A little—before supper.

LENA

It didn't spoil your appetite.

LOGAN

No'm. I'm trained to eat under fire.

LENA

Was it that bad?

LOGAN

(*Thinks*) At first. (*Nods*)

LENA

I'm sorry. It was Paul's idea, not mine.

LOGAN

See, I miss my mother—I told you that. I tried not to say a real goodbye to her when I left for Idaho—she was such a deep worrier—so now all I've got is: *she's* the one that's pulled out and left me standing on the platform waving and hoping she'll look back one last time.

LENA

She would, if they'd give her the chance. But my aunt used to say, "When they take you fast, they're proving they love you."

LOGAN

(*Thinks*) They must be nuts about young boys then.

LENA

I said you'd be safe. I know it in my bones.

LOGAN

(*Studies her, smiles slightly, nods*) Then I won't doubt your word.

LENA

—Lena. Call me Lena please.

LOGAN

All right. (*Waits, swallows coffee*) Lena—what did my mother know about you?

LENA *has dreaded that but takes it almost calmly. She reaches for a student paper. On its clean back she begins writing lines of Palmer-Method exercises—circles and spikes.*

LENA

Paul used to say *nothing*. She'd never asked a question or showed a sign of worry. That was way back at the start. I haven't asked—oh—since Gail learned to talk.

LOGAN

He was right—it never changed. She'd have told me if she'd known.

LENA

(*Scrawls a moment more, then looks up*) I won't doubt your word. (*Smiles*) But it's hard *not* to. All my life I've had this curse— (*Quickly she cups hands over her eyes, then uncovers them again*) I can see through time. Maybe it comes from working with children all my adult life; but I know what people think, whatever they tell me.

LOGAN

And you've told *me* the truth?

LENA

(*Nods*) You'll never leave Idaho, except to come home.

LOGAN

Then what's he thinking? (*Points toward the living room*)

LENA

Paul? He's numb right now—I don't mean his nap. He loved your mother too. He'll be lost for a while. Then he'll ask my opinion.

LOGAN

On what?

LENA

Where his home is, how he'll live from here on.

LOGAN

He'll move here with you.

LENA

(*Thinks, shakes her head*) Too many questions here. There's plenty little towns to get lost in. They all have schools; all need pianos. (*Smiles*)

LOGAN

Do you want that?—moving again, seeing more of Paul, a family Christmas?

LENA

(*Thinks*) Funny *you* should ask. Paul never has. For all I know, he may not.

LOGAN

He will. He told me. He wanted my blessing.

LENA

That was too much to ask you—*this* week, at least.

LOGAN

He's always assumed I was strong as he. He means it as a compliment.

LENA

You will be.

LOGAN

I am.

LENA

(*Nods unsmiling*) Did you bless him then?

LOGAN *takes a swallow of coffee. Then—almost somnambulistic—he rises, goes to the sink, empties the cup, runs water till it's cold. Then he bends and drinks directly from the stream. He stands, dries his lips with the back of his hand, and stares out the window toward the dimly-lit yard.*

LOGAN

Not yet, I don't guess.

LENA

Is my coffee that bad? (*Smiles*)

LOGAN

(*His back still to* LENA) No, I was thirsty. (*Turns and faces her, studies her face*) How have you borne this?

LENA

I won't say it's been my favorite *day.*

LOGAN

I meant the whole last—what?—seventeen years.

LENA

I'm tough and not too bright.

LOGAN

Both lies. I can *see.* (*Touches his eyes*)

LENA

Well, I told them to myself—nobody else till you.

LOGAN

You've been claiming to tell me trustworthy facts.

LENA

(*Thinks, nods*) Excuse me. O.K. This is bedrock *fact*—
it's been so bad at times I'd have killed myself if there
hadn't been Gail.

LOGAN

He'd have seen to Gail.

LENA

He wouldn't. He told me. See, I tried it once. The Christmas she was two years old and asked for him—the next
time he stopped here, I *went* for myself.

She holds up her left wrist—a long white scar.

LOGAN *studies it from a distance. Then he slowly comes to the table, sits, and extends a finger to touch the scar.*

LENA *takes it back and wipes it on her lips.*

LENA

As soon as the blood stopped, he sat me down right here at this table and said, very calmly, "You were grown when you met me. You knew my life but you took me on. Gail followed from that. If you plan to leave her, find a home for her first—she can't come with me."

LOGAN

He said it that plain?

LENA

Verbatim, more or less.

LOGAN

And you stayed on.

LENA

I guess I did. (*Again she rubs the scarred wrist, with her right hand*) I seem to be the same person anyhow, most days.

LOGAN

(*Shakes his head*) God—

LENA

I haven't finished yet. (*Smiles*) You asked for the truth.
Why I'm *here* at all—why Gail is in my room conjugat-
ing Latin—is because Paul Melton is asleep on the couch
in that dark living-room. (*Points*) He's a gentle person,
with the time he's had. And he's all I've wanted. Something put me in his path nearly half my life ago. We've
enjoyed each other, whoever we hurt. And *we'll* pay for
that, nobody else now.

LOGAN

What about Gail and me?

LENA

Gail'll be gone soon—two or three more years—some boy
of her own. I can't stop that. (*Waits, searches* LOGAN's
eyes) You've gone already—on your own life, I mean.
You're strong as us or stronger. If we ever hurt you, it's
over now.

LOGAN

(*Nods*) I hope you're right. (*Waits, then smiles*) You
throwing us out?

LENA

(*Quickly*) Lord, no. You're welcome wherever we are—
if we end up together.

LOGAN

You will. Paul Melton can't stay alone long.

LENA

I don't know that. Anything else he's wanted, he's managed to have. Being lonely is just a simple skill. You can learn it if you want to.

LOGAN

I don't think I do.

LENA

(*Serious*) I didn't mean you. I just preach to *myself*.

LOGAN

(*Smiles*) In what church? I'd like to join your church.

LENA

(*Begins to calm*) I call it The Church of Getting Through Time. No, Gail goes along to the Methodists sometime. I don't have the gall.

They do not know it yet, but they have answered their questions about one another. The stream between them runs relatively clear.

LOGAN *pushes back from the table with his hands, rocks on the hind legs of his chair, and stares up at the ceiling —the dim warm flicker of shadow from the lamp.*

LENA *reaches for the papers again and begins to sort them.*

LOGAN *looks down at last.*

LOGAN

I'll leave you to work.

LENA

(*Smiles*) Where would you go?—we've got a full house.

LOGAN

I'll wake Dad up. (*Looks to his watch*) We can listen to the news.

LENA

I could fix you a snack.

LOGAN

(*Standing*) You grade your papers. Maybe after that.

LENA *nods and reaches to take her red pencil.*

LOGAN *moves toward the hall door. He stops on the threshold and turns back to* LENA.

Her eyes are still on him.

LENA

I haven't lied to you.

LOGAN

I believe you. I'll be back.

He turns again and takes three steps into the dark hall. Then he stops and returns.

LENA *still faces him.*

LOGAN
You know I loved my mother?

LENA
It's one of the main things I'll know from now on.

LOGAN *waits a moment, nods, gives a little parting wave, and leaves again.*

LENA *watches him out of sight, then turns up her lamp and takes a student paper.*

23

Immediately after in LENA's *living room.* LOGAN *comes to the open door and stops, the dim hall behind him.*

The living room is only lit by the filtered shine from a street lamp. PAUL *is on the sofa—on his back, his head propped awkwardly on an old felt pillow. His face is obscured, and* LOGAN *cannot be sure he's asleep.*

LOGAN
(*Half-volume, from the doorway*) Dad?

No answer. PAUL *doesn't move.*

LOGAN
(*Slightly louder*) Sir—

PAUL's *hand flicks once at his face—a fly—but still no answer. Then a thin strain of snoring grinds out.*

LOGAN *smiles, takes a step in, and looks round the room —a small upright piano in a corner.* LOGAN *silently moves*

toward it and sits on the bench. He looks once more to
PAUL—*still snoring. Then he turns to the keys, poises a*
moment, and begins the Chopin Prelude in D Flat (the
one GAIL *had played). He plays it note-perfect, deeply*
felt. The entire piece consumes a little more than four
minutes. In its course, and responding to its varying
moods, the following silent actions occur.

PAUL *gradually wakes, looks over to* LOGAN, *studies his*
profile, then sits up and rubs his own eyes. He rises and
goes to stand behind LOGAN. *He is close but does not*
touch him.

In the "Raindrop" passage, GAIL *appears in the doorway.*
She stops there—disheveled from studying—and watch-
es the two men's backs. Her face is nearly blank. Neither
PAUL *nor* LOGAN *turn to see her.*

A few seconds from the end of the piece, LENA *appears.*
She stops behind GAIL, *again not touching, and listens*
calmly.

At the last note, LOGAN's *hands stay on the keys. He has*
sensed his father's nearness but has not heard the
women.

PAUL
(*In place, not moving*) She'd have been very proud.

LOGAN
(*To the keys*) I practice when I can.

PAUL *opens his right hand and lays it broadly on the crown of* LOGAN's *head.*

LOGAN *does not turn but shuts his eyes and smiles very slightly.*

GAIL *gently applauds.*

LENA *moves to restrain her.*

PAUL *looks back;* LOGAN *does not.*

>   PAUL
Is it *day* already?

GAIL *turns to* LENA.

LENA *takes a step forward.*

LOGAN *turns on the bench and looks back.*

>   LENA
(*Shakes her head*) Barely bedtime. That was beautiful, Logan.

LOGAN *nods acceptance.*

>   LENA
I promised you a snack.

>   PAUL
Any walnut pie left?

LENA

Not a crumb.

PAUL

Any eggs?

LENA

Two dozen—

PAUL

I'll make a cheese omelet.

GAIL

Then *nobody* would sleep.

PAUL *smiles and begins to move toward the door.*

PAUL

Nothing wrong with that—sleep's a big superstition; you been saying so for years.

He passes the women and vanishes toward the kitchen.

LENA *watches his back in mild exasperation, then follows him.*

GAIL *and* LOGAN *face each other. He stays on the bench.*

GAIL *advances to the center of the room.*

LOGAN *takes another long look at her face. Then he slowly turns to the keys again and plays the Bach Prelude in C.*

REYNOLDS PRICE

Born in Macon, North Carolina in 1933, Reynolds
Price attended North Carolina schools and re-
ceived his Bachelor of Arts degree from Duke Uni-
versity. As a Rhodes Scholar he studied for three
years at Merton College, Oxford, receiving the
Bachelor of Letters with a thesis on Milton. In
1958 he returned to Duke where he is now James
B. Duke Professor of English. His first novel *A
Long and Happy Life* appeared in 1962. A volume
of stories *The Names and Faces of Heroes* appeared in 1963. In the years since, he has published
A Generous Man (a novel), *Love and Work* (a
novel), *Permanent Errors* (stories), *Things Them-
selves* (essays and scenes), *The Surface of Earth*
(a novel), *Early Dark* (a play), *A Palpable God*
(translations from the Bible with an essay on the
origins and life of narrative), *The Source of Light*
(a novel), and *Vital Provisions* (poems). His first
two novels and the story "A Chain of Love" are
now collected in a single volume, *Mustian*. His
books have been translated into fourteen lan-
guages.